Beckham and the Conquest of America

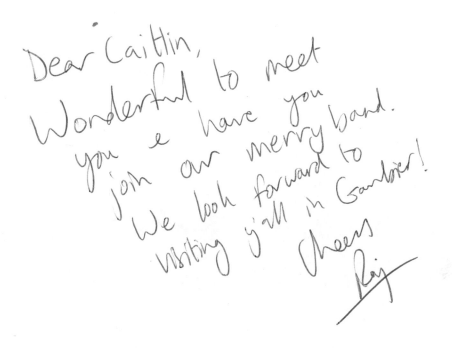

Dear Caitlin,
Wonderful to meet
you & have you
join our merry band.
We look forward to
visiting y'all in Gardner!
Cheers
Raj

Beckham and the Conquest of America

✦

Raj Purohit

iUniverse, Inc.
New York   Bloomington

Beckham and the Conquest of America

iUniverse books may be ordered through booksellers or by contacting:

iUniverse
1663 Liberty Drive
Bloomington, IN 47403
www.iuniverse.com
1-800-Authors (1-800-288-4677)

ISBN: 978-0-595-52853-0 (pbk)
ISBN: 978-0-595-62907-7 (ebk)

Printed in the United States of America

iUniverse rev. date: 12/5/2008

Dedication

This book is for my wife, parents and sister - thanks for your love and support. Also a big thanks to my good mate Tom Moran for all the advice and editing assistance - cheers!

Note from the author

I am writing this book in real time, or as close to real time as I can. My objective is to marry the "blogging" formula with that of a conventional book or diary. Unlike mosaics of the past, please remember that pieces of this one were created before I was clear what the final picture would show. This chronicle, this blog-diary, is perhaps unusual in style, but seeks to reflect and harness the approach to information in the 21st Century. I hope you enjoy these reflections on Beckham, that they help paint a picture of his first year engaging with MLS and that in true blog style that you find ways to join the conversation.

My hope is that I will be able to construct a mosaic that illustrates how David Beckham began his conquest of America. This book is Part 1 of that conquest but with every journey there needs to be a beginning. And here it is.

Table of Contents

New Beginnings

When David Beckham announced on January 11, 2007 that he would be swapping the glamour of Real Madrid and La Liga for LA Galaxy and the Major League Soccer (MLS), many pundits in Europe and across the globe suggested that it heralded the end of an era. The feeling among those "in the know" was that he had called time on a career at the highest levels because he could no longer "cut it". The rap on Beckham was that he had lost some of his desire for the game and that he was no longer the all action player who had won a hat full of domestic and European titles with Manchester United. After all, the right-sided midfielder had in short order lost the captaincy of his country, his place in the national side and his starting spot for Los Merengues (Real Madrid). Adding insult to injury, he had been dropped from the Real Madrid squad the week before the Galaxy announcement by the club's coach Fabio Capello. Consequently, the move to MLS was seen as a smart financial decision for the Beckham brand while alluding to a recognition that Beckham-the-soccer-player was ready for semi-retirement. The decision by Real to initially offer a contract extension did not change this narrative.

Although the leadership at Real had offered Beckham a two-year extension to his current deal, it was perceived by many observers, and perhaps the player himself, that the offer was an economic decision and not a move to secure the services of an on-field star. Beckham had been worth millions of dollars per year to Real Madrid since his transfer from Manchester United in the summer of 2003. Estimates of his "value" to the club off the field varied but a mid-range figure of $40 million seemed reasonable.

Beckham himself was almost certainly aware of the thinking behind the Real Madrid offer and the feeling among soccer pundits that he was past his prime. Observers of Beckham should not have been surprised that he would set about seeking to prove the doubters wrong. David Beckham the man is blessed with mental strength and a confidence in his own ability. He is also a man who loves the game as much as anyone who has played it – whether in a park or at the World Cup. The hierarchy at Real failed to recognize this fact and consequently they were probably somewhat surprised when he turned down their offer and instead joined the LA Galaxy. Pundits across the soccer world were also in for a surprise when Beckham then dug deep and emerged from the battering he took from the press to recommit himself to Real's title challenge.

When Beckham claimed that he would commit to working hard for his club for the remainder of the season few believed him. And yet, as I write here on June 17th 2007, David Beckham is heading to the MLS with a prized La Liga medal, the profound respect of his Madrid team and the adulation of the Madrid fans. As a consequence, Real Madrid's hierarchy tried desperately to keep him at the club but to no avail. Similarly, now that he has been reinstated to the English national team, the English soccer punditocracy has been worrying aloud about the impact flying will have on their midfielder.

It is the LA Galaxy organization that looked very smart in the aftermath of the title win; in late 2006-early 2007 they remembered what many pundits worldwide had forgotten - David Beckham is a talented soccer player who lives and breathes the game.

The day after Real's win he was on the front cover of USA Today - for the right reasons. He is, again, a winner and the MLS is the next frontier for him to conquer.

This book is about Beckham's initial effort to conquer America. But if the challenge and the possibility of success are to be fully understood, we need to understand how he fits into the thinking of the MLS leadership group. We need to grasp the complexities of Beckham the man as well as Beckham the player while simultaneously considering the challenges facing him. But before we examine how he has started this conquest, we also need to consider what happened in the weeks and months after the LA Galaxy deal was announced, for the journey began on the other side of the Atlantic, in Spain.

Beckham and the Beginning of the Title Drive

It has been said that it is always darkest before the dawn, and so it proved to be this season for the eventual La Liga champions and for their midfielder David Beckham.

For Real Madrid the season was, perhaps, at its darkest when they lost 1-0 to Levante in a game that was slated to be a historic celebration at their home stadium, the Santiago Bernabéu. The Levante game was to be the time for a tremendous celebration to herald the one thousandth league match played there. Unfortunately the champagne was kept on ice as a Real Madrid team, with Raul ensconced on the right side of midfield, was unable to break down Levante. Raul tried to show some leadership from his right sided position; unfortunately, although he showed some decent moves, he was unable to provide the spark Real needed to win such a historic game.

David Beckham did not play that night; he was not in the team for the Levante game. Fabio Capello, Real's legendary Italian coach, was still of the mind that Beckham should never play for the team again – he had publicly stated that the LA Galaxy move effectively precluded Beckham from playing a role for the remainder of the season. Interestingly, it was the senior players at Real who were responsible for Capello's eventual reversal. Led by the current captain and probable future President of Real Madrid, Raul, the group met with Capello and urged him to bring Beckham back into the fold. They managed to take advantage of Capello's weak position with the Madrid faithful and pressure him into changing course.

This was accomplished, in part, by leaking to the press that the senior players had urged Capello to rethink. Suddenly the seasoned coach was left with little option but to bring Beckham back for the game against Real Sociedad.

Such an overt display of player power tends to be rare in the world of soccer.

Certainly few would have predicted that Beckham's fate would be decided by such a political move from his fellow players. English national team fans may remember that in 1990 a senior delegation of players forced then coach Bobby Robson to include Mark Wright as a sweeper for key group games but such incidents tend to be few and far between. Nevertheless, all supporters of Real Madrid will forever be thankful that player-power won out in this instance. It allowed David Beckham to go from a player marginalized first by country and then club to get back into the fray and to attempt to secure glory in Spain before the move to the United States. Beckham himself deserves much of the credit for this move. He acted honorably and with dignity after the visceral reaction of Capello and the Real Madrid hierarchy to the Galaxy deal. He remained calm, showed that he was "tranquilo" and stated that he was ready to help the team. He was ready to do the job he was paid to carry out. This helped build a base of support for action among the players and the fans.

And so, with Capello reinstating Beckham to the side for the game against Real Sociedad, it was perhaps fitting that Beckham scored a goal with one of his trade-mark free kicks from outside the area. Admittedly, the wet turf aided him as the goalkeeper failed to stop a kick that he probably should have saved. Nevertheless, Beckham had his goal and Madrid had a critical victory that at least righted their ship after the defeat by Levante. Although few would have bet on a title win at the time, it was the beginning of Madrid's Beckham inspired push to their 30th La Liga.

Lalas v the English Premier League (EPL) "Supporters" club

In the aftermath of Beckham's last game for Real Madrid, a core group of English journalists stepped up their public critique of Major League Soccer. The amalgamated complaint raised by these reporters was that Beckham would be playing in an inferior league and would therefore be unable to maintain his high standards for the national side. Some of these writers seemed to be hoping that the escape clause in Beckham's contract was real to protect him from this soccer backwater; others suggested that a loan deal during the MLS off-season may be the best way to ensure Beckham remained competitive enough for Euro 2008 and beyond.

Putting aside the hypocrisy of such "concerns" from many reporters who had been so quick to write off Beckham's international prospects earlier in the year, and that some had almost gleefully written his international obituary, these remarks were perceived as incredibly damaging by the leadership of MLS.

Nevertheless, many of the senior figures within the game declined to get involved in a slanging match with commentators whose self-interest saw them talk up the EPL over other leagues. One individual took a different path; Alexi Lalas, the President of the LA Galaxy, happily joined the fray.

Lalas has always been a colorful character from the days when he burst onto the world soccer scene as a goatee wearing, guitar playing hardnosed defender. In recent years he has redefined himself as part of the new leadership of US soccer. Lalas, perhaps predictably, clearly felt that he needed to respond to the shots being leveled at his team and league; he also probably saw an opportunity to garner some earned media coverage.

To that end, he gave a long interview with the British based Guardian newspaper (the Guardian has significant readership in the US via its website and new US edition), the interview was featured online, and included a series of choice comments.

On the quality contrast between the EPL and MLS Lalas stated:

"In England, our league is considered second class, but I honestly believe if you took a helicopter and grabbed a bunch of MLS players and took them to the perceived best league in the world they wouldn't miss a beat and the fans wouldn't notice any drop in quality."

On the EPL itself:

"The fact that a segment of the world worships an inferior product in the Premiership is their business."

To be fair to Lalas, some of his comments were taken a little out of context. He cleverly contrasted La Liga with the EPL in order to take some shots at the league being covered by the journalists who were bashing MLS.... in a sense this was Lalas' way of saying to those commentators, "people in glass houses shouldn't throw stones," or to put it another way, "if you are going to bash the MLS for relying on the glitz of Beckham, consider the reasons why your own league is the most viewed in the world - is it really the best or is it clever marketing?"

Lalas seemingly made his comments for a number of interconnected reasons but at its core these comments were designed to convey a message to American futbol fans that the MLS understood that the Beckham deal has given it an opportunity to systematically build the base of support for the league and to improve the brand. Lalas wanted to show that he was ready to fight for the league and was the perfect ally for David Beckham as he sought to conquer America.

Gavin Hamilton: Dead Wrong About Beckham's Impact on Real Title Surge

Gavin Hamilton, the editor in chief of World Soccer Magazine, is a real opinion shaper of the sport globally. His columns in the magazine and for CNN.com tend to be insightful and make clear that he has a good feel for the game. This reality made his column on the significance, or lack thereof, of Beckham's contribution to the Real title charge a very surprising one. Hamilton contended, in his CNN online column of June 18th, that Beckham was far from being a key influence on the title surge:

"Ultimately, Real won the Spanish league title due to a number of factors, all of which were more important than Beckham's form and fitness. Barcelona suffered a disastrous drop in form and Real was able to take advantage. Capello's training regime improved players' fitness levels and helped Madrid secure late victories in matches which it had lost in previous seasons. As for individuals, 25-goal striker Ruud van Nistelrooy and goalkeeper Iker Casillas were far more important than Beckham."

Hamilton's desire to diminish Beckham's contribution was surprising, particularly because the Madrid faithful and Beckham's own team clearly felt that he had a critical role to play in the surge for La Liga.

It was also very odd to see him start that column with this statement from late Man Utd legend George Best:

"David Beckham isn't a great. He can't kick with his left foot, he can't tackle, he doesn't head the ball and he doesn't score many goals. Apart from that, he's all right."

Reflecting on these comments, supporters of Beckham could be forgiven for questioning what their man needed to do to ensure he was given credit from the futbol punditocracy - Beckham had bounced back in incredible fashion from the nadir that threatened to envelope him just before the Galaxy deal was announced. He was leaving for LA with a La Liga winner's medal, the praise of Madrid's legions of fans and the knowledge that he was still wanted at the Bernabeau. And yet he could not get the praise from key soccer pundits that his play deserved.

Beckham's fans and inner circle understand how important respect is to the midfielder and on the dawn of a new challenge some may have worried if it would make him doubt whether it was the right time to leave Europe. Did the player feel as if he still had something to prove? Fortunately there were no signs that this was the case and those same supporters could take solace from the fact that, for every column by pundits like Hamilton, there were positive statements from those who perhaps new Beckham's game the best - his current and former teammates.

Seemingly addressing the Beckham legacy at almost the same time Hamilton was writing, the legendary Real Madrid and French star Zinadine Zidane (aka Zizou) stated in a Sunday Mirror interview that: "David is immortalized in football history. He is one of the game's greatest players."

Winning over Casillas

"It's annoying there's so much talk of Beckham when we're competing for the league....Besides, I can't really imagine him at this club. He's more about marketing than football." ---- Real Madrid and Spain first choice goalkeeper Iker Casillas.

Fact: Iker Casillas rarely seems short of an opinion.

Fact: He was not particularly happy when stories of Beckham joining Real, and potentially displacing his friend Luis Figo, surfaced just as Real closed in on their 29th title.

Fact: As Beckham got ready to leave the club at the end of the season, Casillas remarked that he would be sad to see him leave and noted that Beckham's qualities had played a key role in Real Madrid's fight for the La Liga title.

Those unfamiliar with the intricacies of the Beckham-Real Madrid story may wonder what can be gleaned from the interaction between Beckham and Casillas and what this has to do with Beckham's conquest of America.

Put simply, the mountain that Beckham had to climb when he joined Real Madrid was a very high one. While his marketing potential was clear to then President of Real Mr. Perez, he was faced with joining a winning team comprised of top quality international performers. Messer's Figo, Zidane, Raul, Ronaldo, Carlos, Guti and of course Casillas were at the height of their collective powers and were not likely to be impressed by a "clothes horse." Additionally, the Real Madrid fans are a knowledgeable group that expected their team to win and to win with style. Beckham could not, even had he desired, joined Real Madrid and coasted. He needed to perform on the pitch to ensure that his teammates did not turn on him and he needed to show the fans that he was fit to wear the white jersey of Real. We know now that Beckham passed both tests with conviction.

Teammates from Casillas to Raul (who urged that Beckham be restored to the squad when Capello banished him from the first team group in January) and Figo (who returned to participate in Beckham's farewell dinner in Madrid) were won over by his humble demeanor, respect for the club and his teammates, his hard work in training and performance on the pitch. Perhaps the most notable praise came from former teammate and true soccer icon Zinedine Zidane. At the end of Beckham's final season with Real Madrid Zizou noted that "David is immortalised in football history. He is one of the game's greatest players." In an interview with the British Sunday Mirror he made it clear that Beckham was driven away from Real and into the thankful arms of the Galaxy:

"The damage had already been done, they should have done more to keep him. There was never any doubt in my mind that he wanted to end his career at the club. But what is the point of staying somewhere you're clearly not wanted? Is it a big mistake? Absolutely. I think Madrid should have done everything in their power to keep him because he's unique. They won't find it easy to replace him - it's almost impossible."

Zizou's comments made clear that Beckham had shown an ability to work hard and stay focused, under immense pressure, and win over even the toughest crowd – the Real Madrid dressing room.

Real Madrid and the Beckham Brand

Without question the possibility of leveraging the Beckham brand to grow soccer in the US was a key consideration for the LA Galaxy when they decided to try and land the former England captain. The Galaxy hierarchy knew that since his move from Manchester United to Real Madrid, the David Beckham brand had grown considerably on the global stage. More significantly, his brand had also ensured significant exposure for Real Madrid and, as a consequence, significant financial gain for the Spanish club. As John Carlin, author of White Angels: Beckham, Real Madrid and the New Football, wrote in the Independent Newspaper:

"The reasons for Real's commercial success are complex, and worthy of specialised study. (Harvard Business School has, in fact, produced a paper on the subject.) But if you had to identify one factor that summed it all up it would have to be contained in two of the world's most famous words: David Beckham."

Carlin understood that Real Madrid has successfully leveraged the Beckham brand not simply because he was a big name in the sport and a terrific player but that he was a "brand" that triggered benefits for their own brand. This type of relationship, where one brand is boosted by its connection to another, is reminiscent of the Michael Jordan effect – an effect that still sees the greatest ever basketball player endorse products ranging from sports apparel to underwear.

By the way, you should get White Angels: Beckham, Real Madrid and the New Football, by John Carlin – it is a good read – and if you want a detailed preview check out the extract in the Sunday Times...I learnt a lot from it!

Beckham's Impact on Real Madrid

Prior to Beckham's July 13th 2007 arrival in LA, the Beckham brand had already shown signs of boosting the MLS. Shirt sales were up 300% from the year before and season ticket sales at the Galaxy had gone through the roof.

All of this was, to a degree, predictable to anyone who had closely followed the impact of Beckham's 20 million pound move from Manchester United to Real Madrid. While the deal was seen as good for both parties by most casual observers, it was especially so for Real Madrid and in particular their marketing director Jose Angel Sanchez. As Carlin reported in his book as well as in the Independent and Sunday Times, Sanchez claimed that the word that kept ringing in his head during the negotiations with then Manchester United Chief Executive Peter Kenyon (now the top man at Chelsea) was "Peanuts! Peanuts! Peanuts!" Carlin also reported that Sanchez went into the meeting with Kenyon willing to pay double the final amount. He believed that Beckham was worth five hundred million euros to Real Madrid.

Sanchez was absolutely right – Beckham would be worth a fortune to Real. By the end of his first winter at Real, Beckham shirts had outsold the rest of the Real Galacticos combined and Real's overall shirt sales had doubled from 2002. Sanchez has stated that Beckham has been worth at least 300 million pounds to Real in marketing revenue. The Times (UK) broke down the Beckham effect quite well:

The Real deal: Beckham¢s effect - Real¢s director of marketing, Jose Angel Sanchez, says Beckham, who cost the club £25m, has been worth more than £300m in marketing revenue to the club. More than one million Beckham shirts were sold during his first six months at the club, and Real recouped his transfer fee in shirt sales during his first season. Revenue from club merchandise jumped 67% that year. In the two years after Beckham joined, Madrid¢s annual sponsorship and advertising income soared 137% to £30m as it improved contracts with the likes of Siemens and Adidas. Sales of jerseys and other merchandising jumped 61.5% to £36m.

Real money: how it breaks down Commercial income from merchandise and sponsorship is worth almost 80 million pounds a year, which equates to 42% of income. In 2000, this figure was lower than 10%. Other major revenue streams include match day income (mainly tickets) of 48 million pounds; television income of 44 million pounds; and 16 million pounds from friendlies and tours. Europe¢s Deloitte Football Money League was headed by Manchester United for eight years from its inception in 1997 until dislodged by Real Madrid in 2004-05.

Real were top last season with 202 million pounds. Barcelona were second (179.1 million pounds) and Juventus third (173.7 million pounds)

This type of pulling power led to Real Madrid finally unseating Manchester United at the top of the Deloitte Football Money League for the 2004/05 season (this is a terrific resource for all soccer fans!)

Rank Club Income

(€ million) Country 1. Real Madrid 275.7 Spain

2. Manchester United 246.4 England

3. A.C. Milan 234.0 Italy

In 2005/06 they increased their income further still:

1. Real Madrid 292.2 Spain

2. FC Barcelona 259.1 Spain

3. Juventus 251.2 Italy

These numbers undoubtedly played an important role in Beckham being recruited by the LA Galaxy. However, it is also fair to say that the Galaxy knew what they were getting in Beckham the player. For all the shirts sold and income generated for Real Madrid, it was worth noting that at his final game for Real, a Union Jack banner read: "David, the Bernabéu will always be your home."

Debut Against Chelsea

David Beckham's first game against Chelsea was guaranteed to be well covered whatever the opposition - the fact that the Galaxy orchestrated things to ensure that he was slated to play a power house of European soccer - Chelsea - ensured additional hype was layered onto the event.

Chelsea's top attractions - from coach Jose Mourinho to stars such as Frank Lampard and John Terry - are certainly used to the media spotlight but even they must have been a little surprised by the hundreds of journalists attending what was, after all, a pre-season game.

The game itself was covered by ESPN as part of an MLS special event (it was also the lead story on Sports Center - not a guarantee even for World Cup finals) and the broadcaster cleverly arranged for some additional cameras to track Beckham's movements.

Of course the whole event could have ended in a real anticlimax had Beckham failed to shake off the ankle injury that almost kept him away from the all-star game.

Luckily for the promoters, fans, the Galaxy and Beckham himself, he was able to play for about 15 minutes. In that time he managed to spray the odd beautiful 50+ yard pass and get clobbered by Chelsea midfield signing Steve Sidwell.

Nevertheless, Beckham got through the game in one piece and managed to get some playing time in front of his adoring public - which included California Governor Arnold Schwarzenegger, Eva Longoria (Desperate Housewives TV star and wife of San Antonio Spurs NBA star Tony Parker) and Katie Holmes.

At the end of the game the crowd and TV audience were treated to a brief interview on the field with Beckham (ESPN cut away from a planned commercial to bring it to the public live!), which then lead into Sports Center, featuring the game as the main story. All in all this was a very good evening of work for Beckham.

And with that the first game of Beckham's conquest of America was in the bag - LA lost 1-0 but most observers suspected that this would not mean much over the course of the season. After all, everyone knew that LA now had a player in their ranks who had led Real Madrid to an improbable title drive just before heading stateside - Beckham would breed confidence for the Galaxy and only time would tell whether this, plus his on field talent, would be enough to secure MLS glory.

Beckham and Super Liga

On the heels of the Beckham v Chelsea ESPN game, a busy summer for soccer fans in the United States got a little busier.

For years the game's administrators had longed to replicate the rivalry between the US and Mexican national teams at a club level.

They finally decided that the way to do this was to organize a Champions League style tournament for Mexican and US clubs. Unfortunately the inaugural Super Liga tournament kicked off without Beckham. His ankle injury prevented him from joining his LA Galaxy teammates as they played celebrated Mexican side Pachuta in the first round of Super Liga games. Galaxy seemed inspired by their new signing and turned in a terrific performance to win the game 2-1. The other teams involved included Houston Dynamo, Chivas, FC Dallas, Club America, Morelia and DC United. The format set up by the sponsors was designed to see the top two teams in each group head to a semi final and then to the final. This type of competition was considered to be the first step towards a Champions League style tournament for clubs from the Confederation of North, Central American and Caribbean Association Football (CONCAF) region.

While the new competition was not a direct consequence of the Beckham deal, the fact that he had joined the MLS increased the international interest in the Galaxy and as a consequence, the league as a whole. This type of 'Beckham effect' or Beckham boost was an early sign of the benefit he would bring to the league.

In some respects this type of knock on benefit was reminiscent of a certain basketball player who wore the same number as Beckham - a Mr. Michael Jordan. It was a well reported fact that Jordan boosted the audiences at games that did not include his team – the Chicago Bulls. While the start of Super

Liga was simply too early to make such a case for Beckham, it was fair to note that the inaugural tournament was perhaps getting more publicity than it could have anticipated. Of course, the fact that the Beckham v Chelsea game broke the ESPN highest soccer viewing record was useful.

Club and Country

Beckham's role with England was certainly a key theme during the lead up to his debut for the Galaxy and the intertwining of the player, club and country was certainly predictable.

Beckham had always loved playing for his country and while there were some low moments, including his sending-off against Argentina, his penalty miss against Argentina and a couple of injury impaired performances, he certainly valued being involved in the national set up. The England captaincy was certainly something he cherished and it seemed clear how much moments like "that" free kick against Greece and the penalty against Argentina meant to him.

There was little doubt that he wanted to get 100 caps for his country and Alexi Lalas, the Galaxy President, cleverly made clear before his debut that Beckham could always rely on the support of the Galaxy when it came to national team issues. At a time when top figures in the English game such as Arsenal coach Wenger and then Newcastle chairman Freddy Sheppard were criticizing various aspects of the international game, Lalas' claim that he would be happy to drive Beckham to the airport for England duty was refreshing and must have resonated with the player.

In the days after the Chelsea game, Beckham reflected on the call from England coach Steve McClaren that seemingly put an end to his England career and the approach he, Beckham, took to get his place back. As reported by Euro Sport (and apparently taken from a comment from the ITV program New Beginnings) McClaren's message to Beckham was simple and with hindsight a decision that harmed the England coach's reputation: "In every team there's going to be casualties, and I'm sorry to say you're one of the casualties."

Beckham described his own reaction, after he recovered from the initial shock (he said he was close to tears) in the following way: "At first it wasn't a case of proving him wrong, because I had to come to terms with what had been said and be patient. But after maybe a day or two and speaking to my friends and my family, then it was a case of 'OK, this is the situation, now how do I get myself out of it?'"

The recounting of this story, during a summer in which he had returned gloriously for England, won La Liga with Real Madrid and had just debuted for the Galaxy, was probably not a chance decision. The story was a piece of the emerging US narrative surrounding Beckham - a man who would keep the peace and his head in times of trouble and had the resolve to overcome adversity to return to the top. He also was starting to make people understand that he believed he could in fact fulfill all his responsibilities - to a new club, a new league and a new country.

Describing the importance of playing for England, in the aftermath of playing hurt for Galaxy against Chelsea and at a time when he was selling the league in the US and globally, he certainly conveyed the image of a player who understood what the game gave to him and what he owed it in return.

Perhaps the moral of this story is that Beckham had learned a lesson that his England coach had failed to grasp - honor the game, work hard and be humble.

Galaxy v Chivas of Guadalajara

The second game in the Super Liga tournament for Beckham's LA side was the clash with Chivas of Guadalajara - essentially the parent club of the Galaxy's Los Angeles rival Chivas USA.

The game was held at the LA Colosseum and would have probably been one of the more significant games of the season for Beckham had he been able to play; unfortunately his ankle injury prevented him from contributing anything more than vocal support from the bench.

Interestingly, Galaxy coach Frank Yallop was very keen to talk up Beckham's leadership potential with the club and suggest that he was fast becoming a leader even without much time on the field. In remarks picked up by Fox Soccer Channel, Yallop noted:

"He definitely wanted to come to the game and be on the bench and be involved in the dressing room, so that's obviously very important to us. We're just desperate to get him on the field. The fans, the players and everyone at the club want him to be healthy and ready to step on the field. He's anxious to do that."

Galaxy's 2-1 defeat to Chivas is important to keep in context. For Chivas is a celebrated team and has the type of quality in their side to trouble any club in the world. They have won the Mexican title 11 times and boast some wonderful players including Omar Bravo and Ramon Morales (in fact these two connected for the winning goal). Defeat to Chivas in front of almost 37,000+ fans was no disgrace for the Galaxy and perhaps was a truer reflection of their standing in the sport globally than the game against Chelsea a couple of weeks earlier.

Beckham would likely have felt that he had something to work with following the performance against Chivas and likely would have been further energized to get fit for action. In an interview with the media his coach too suggested that the leadership of Beckham was welcome, needed and would likely pay dividends:

"Abel Xavier has taken it on himself to talk to the back four and work out with our defenders what the best system is. I'm sure David will do the same type of thing with his midfield players and probably the front players too."

Also worth noting was the fact that Beckham, yet again, seemed to be quickly winning over a locker room:

"It's good to have him around. It's a boost of morale for the team because he's right behind us and he's always been from day one, to be honest." said Yallop in the post match comments to the press.

Pele

David Beckham's first weeks in LA were certain to spark a flurry of stories and colorful commentary. In keeping with more than a decade of past coverage of Beckham, one could also have assumed that we would see a combination of positive and negative articles. To a large extent the player would surely have anticipated many of them; particularly the standard critical comments from former professionals ranging from the best and brightest of commentators to a few washed up professionals looking to leverage any tangential connection to Beckham's American adventure to garner some column inches.

Beckham would have been ready for a few negative articles and would likely be prepared to respond on the pitch; after all Beckham has shown that he likes to correct misimpressions using his feet – in that sense he is an old fashioned professional with an approach to soccer debates that can be summed up as head down, mouth shut and get on with it.

Nevertheless Beckham could be forgiven for being a little upset after a sucker punch was thrown at him by the greatest futbol player ever, Pele*. While it only lasted for one or two news cycles, the story is worth noting in any analysis of Beckham's quest to conquer America because it shows the challenges facing the player as soon as he landed in the States.

It was just before the Super Liga game against FC Dallas (Beckham did not play due to an ankle injury) that Pele launched his astonishing attack on the new Galaxy star. He did so via an interview with a German newspaper (Frankfurter Allgemeine Sonntagszeitung). Among the comments leveled at Beckham were the following:

"David Beckham is more of a pop star than a player," Pele told Germany's Frankfurter Allgemeine Sonntagszeitung and "I know the level of play in that league. It is very evenly balanced, and the fans will demand a lot from a star like him. He can stroll through Hollywood on his days off and when he has no training."

Such opinions have to be considered both because of their source - the original Number 10 – and because Pele had made a similar journey to Beckham when he joined the North American Soccer League (NASL) all those years ago. However, it cannot have escaped the notice of Beckham watchers that Pele's comments seemed ill considered and, perhaps, just a little bit odd.

For all Beckham's faults he has always taken the game seriously. His commitment to practice, fitness training and strong work ethic have been the basis for solid and respectful relationships with players like Zidane and Casillas. Sir Alex Ferguson would often tell stories of Beckham, whether as a youngster or a seasoned professional, spending hours working on his free kicks after training. Clearly he is not a player who needs to be told to focus on practice by anyone.

While Beckham wisely kept quiet, he must have wondered why Pele would go out of his way to take shots at him; particularly so soon after he landed in LA and prior to his participation in any meaningful games.

It certainly did not do Pele any favors and some commentators must have wondered why a legend of the game would make comments that seemed to be so uninformed.

Beckham, predictably, did not respond in a public way but surely he would have thought to himself "That is very unfair. Why did Pele make these comments?"

As an aside I have to say that I am sympathetic to the claim by most Argentines that Diego Armando Maradona is, at least, on a par with Pele. I grew up watching Maradona and, despite the fact that I am an England fan, was in awe at the way he led from the front as a good Argentine side won the World Cup in 1986 and a distinctly average Argentine side made it to the final in 1990. Nevertheless, it is Pele who is considered the greatest player ever…although maybe I'll write a book on that one day!

Dale Earnhardt Jr. and Tiger Respect Beckham

One of the fascinating contradictions associated with Beckham is that while he is being criticized by sports writers and other sports figures, he is also vigorously supported by credible stakeholders in global sports.

During the time when Beckham was the subject of some negative group think by various reporters, for issues ranging from the size of his contract to his friends in LA (including Tom Cruise) and his injured ankle, he was receiving high profile praise for his actions both on and off the field.

All American hero and NASCAR star Dale Earnhardt Jr. spent a good part of his Adidas clothes line launch praising Beckham. The Associated Press captured the money quote from Junior, who became just the fourth athlete to have his own clothing line with Adidas, joining Reggie Bush, Tracy McGrady and David Beckham. He said: "I look up to Beckham and the things he's been able to accomplish and the persona he's built up over the years."

A few weeks after Junior's welcome comments it was the turn of Tiger Woods to praise Beckham's impact on global sports. Woods beat Beckham, and a host of other stars, to win an ESPN online poll focusing on the "ultimate sports star."

In comments eagerly picked up by the Times (UK), Woods clearly recognized the global support Beckham receives was not reflected in a poll significantly impacted by American voters and made his feelings clear:

"I don't see how, as far as world athletes are concerned, Beckham didn't beat me. As far as global figures are concerned, he [Beckham] is probably far more global than I am. You know, golf is not truly played all around the world like soccer or football is. I think the whole 'Who's Now' [poll] was just about in America. If it had gone globally, it would probably have been different."

While some may argue that such poll's are just a bit of harmless fun, they do reflect and impact sports stories and opinion. It was interesting to see Tiger Woods go out of his way to praise Beckham's global reach – illustrating again Beckham's ability to win credible sports figures to his side.

DC United v LA Galaxy

Thursday August 9th was a special day for your intrepid author. I had secured my tickets for the DC United v LA Galaxy game many months prior but fully anticipated that Beckham would have played a few MLS games before rolling into Washington.

As it turned out, he had not played a minute of MLS soccer prior to the DC United match. Somewhat unfairly, some reporters were trying to create a negative storyline leading into this game. The accusation leveled at MLS was that casual sports fans were heading to watch the game and if Beckham did not show they would be so disappointed and would not come back.

From the beginning, this story line seemed more than a little suspicious. At Toronto FC for instance, where Beckham was supposed to play his first MLS game, they had seen record sell-out crowds for every single match of the season (their first). Their stadium would have been filled with or without Beckham. Now would those fans have liked to see Beckham? Of course. Was his appearance in a suit on the touchline instead of the field a factor likely to harm their link with Toronto FC - no chance.

So with doubts about the media narrative in mind I went to the DC United game not really thinking that Beckham would play. He had, it was reported, not trained at all and even the attendance of England coach Steve McClaren did not convince me that there was a serious chance he would play any part in the proceedings.

The build up to the game was incredible and highlighted the disconnect between those reporters suggesting that MLS had blown the Beckham roll out of proportion and the real strategy employed by the league. Many writers believe that the objective behind bringing Beckham to the MLS was to pull sports fans into the stadium and then convert them into soccer fans. However, it seems that MLS has a different plan in mind – that is to bring the millions of soccer fans in the country into positive contact with the MLS.

And on this summer night in August the plan looked like it was working perfectly. It really was a terrific evening at RFK - the stadium was rocking as the fans came out to celebrate the arrival of Beckham AND to support their home town team.

And that was the key point, yes there were a lot of fans at this specific game because of the former England captain BUT it was very hard to spot any first time soccer fans. Instead it seemed to be a situation where people who come to watch DC United from time to time made sure they came to the game -- and by doing so they really had a fun evening.

Anyone who attended that game would have realized that it showcased the real beauty of the Beckham deal. It was clear that he would not be taking NFL fans and turning them into soccer fans; what he was going to do was encourage soccer fans and MLS fans to make a point of coming to the game. Two of my pals provide a good illustration of the way the Beckham effect could work. Both had previously been to DC United before and enjoyed themselves BUT because they know they can get a ticket anytime they don't really get around to coming out. But for Beckham they made sure they came out and they loved being part of the 45,000 crowd. They will be back again.

It was at the very beginning of the match that the fans in attendance thought that they might just see the former England captain play a few minutes. Beckham walked out with the rest of the LA Galaxy substitutes to cheers (and a few light hearted jeers from the DCU Screaming Eagles) and flashing cameras. Those cheers and flashing cameras were replicated throughout the first half as Beckham jogged, stretched and generally warmed up.

Would he play or wouldn't he? That was a question fans asked each other as they sat back and enjoyed a strong performance from their hometown team. Some fans felt DC United's good play increased the chances of Beckham playing. Others had their doubts as the clouds opened and RFK was soaked in a torrential down pour (Beckham would later confirm to the media what District residents may know – we have BIG rain! He noted that "..it was just the biggest raindrops I've ever seen..."

The players came out and the status quo remained - Beckham was still warming up; DC United was still playing well and the LA Galaxy needed a lift. And then it happened - roars and screams from the crowd closest to Becks, the crowd getting to their feet – an electric atmosphere where team loyalty was forgotten (with the exception of the lusty booing coming from the Screaming Eagles/ Barra Brava sections) and suddenly 45,000 plus knew that at that precise moment they were at the center of the soccer universe; they were seeing a bit of history as David Beckham took to the field.

20 minutes later it was all over - DC had won 1-0, the fans were happy and the Beckham effect had been beautifully illustrated. Beckham himself seemed fairly relaxed at the end of the night and didn't seem keen to build the performance up too much. Talking with reporters he noted:

"Obviously, there's been a certain amount of pressure because everyone is talking about how I've come to MLS and not played yet... but I don't feel pressure in that sense. I feel pressure in myself to get fit and to get back playing again."

A nice touch at the end of the game was Beckham swapping shirts with DC United icon Ben Olsen. Olsen had been supportive of Beckham earlier in the week and after the match stated "I give him a lot of credit for playing because I know he's not 100 percent... he knew a lot of people were here to watch him and he gritted it out and played."

New England and The Critics

It was, perhaps, just another week in the life of David Beckham. After his brief appearance against DC United at RFK, he was criticized in various quarters for his no show against the New England Revolution. From the BBC to reputable US main stream media, the story line that started to gain momentum was one of Beckham failing to live up to the hype (the 2nd time in a month that the story line surfaced). Predictably some media types, a few with more to gain from seeing Beckham fail than succeed, started to say he was a non-story (of course if they were saying this for a new piece they were contradicting themselves!).

Beckham himself was forced to defend his lack of playing time by correctly noting that his no shows have been based on an injury, nothing else, and that he would be ready to play as soon as it was healed.

While Beckham's words were not enough to keep the media hounds at bay, observers of the player would have anticipated that he would find a way to bounce back in the way he always has - on the field.

Unfortunately Beckham could not immediately build on his cameo performance against DC United as the Galaxy's east coast swing took them to New England.

The midfielder had slightly aggravated his ankle in the 1-0 defeat at RFK. There seemed to be some understanding from the fans - in an AP article by Jimmy Golen, the maturity of the fan base being targeted by MLS was illustrated:

"I think everyone wanted to see him play. But we're all big soccer fans, so it's just nice to be here and see so many people at a professional soccer game," said Joan Hopkins, who came with her daughter and three buses full of fans from the Portland, Maine, area. "Hopefully the interest in David Beckham will help build momentum in the popularity of the sport."

Unfortunately many reporters were not so forgiving of his decision to sit out the match. Several articles ran after the New England game suggesting that Beckham and MLS were in danger of blowing the roll out plan.

Even the BBC got caught up in the negativity; they ran a piece under a "Beckham Backlash" heading with these choice comments from Peter Bowes, the BBC's news correspondent in Los Angeles:

"A month ago they were the talk of the town during the relatively quiet mid-summer period. But now with all this uncertainty surrounding Beckham and competition from other sports as we move into the autumn, there is the sense that they have blown it in terms of capitalising on that surge of initial publicity."

He went on to suggest that Beckham simply needed to appear in the very near future or else....

Despite the fact that Beckham had yet to start a game, these comments seemed a little bit too pessimistic. As the player himself had noted - he was going to be in the US for a long time, a few missed games here or there would not break the campaign to conquer America.

Nevertheless, from Beckham to Lalas and the entire LA Galaxy organization, the pressure for Beckham to play became a little bit more pronounced.

After Foxboro (but before New York)

After Beckham failed to play against the New England Revolution at Foxboro, Boston Globe columnist Alex Beam wrote a no-holds barred piece titled "Meanwhile: Beckham hype won't play in the US" in which he sought to make clear why Beckham would not succeed in attempting to conquer America - or as Beam put it:

"Here are three reasons why the hype-fueled, micro-marketed, "Americanization of David Beckham" - the title of a splashy Vanity Fair cover story - will fail"

Beam's list was comprised of these three issues: It Can't Happen Here (because the road to soccer glory does not run through the United States); The Soccer Angle (the sport will not crack the top 5 US sports and Americans are lost on the subtleties); Posh isn't playing (enough said).

I want to focus on the first two because it is frustratingly clear that many people with valuable column space to utilize write about Beckham and MLS without understanding the dynamics at play.

First, Beam fails to understand that soccer already runs through America. Millions play the sport, the top teams come to the US to play in the summer and draw good crowds, multiple TV channels cover the game, the US is among the favorites to host World Cup 2014 or the one after, and the fan base is growing in both numbers and sophistication.

Second, MLS does not need to convert fans from another sport to soccer – their objective is to take some of the millions of soccer fans in the country and turn them into diehard MLS fans. Becoming the

3rd, 4th or 5th sport is not relevant. The objective is to build steadily and bring in those who love the sport already.

Beckham helps with both counts – he brings in casual fans and, much more significantly, soccer fans with a casual understanding of MLS. I saw this first hand at DC United and we will see more of this in the months ahead.

DC United in the Super Liga

In the Super Liga game against DC United, Beckham took center stage and proved that stories of his demise were exaggerated. Beckham started to make news from the pre-game when he came out as captain - for a minute it seemed that controversy would swirl around Beckham's first start; surely his coach Frank Yallop had not forcibly pulled the golden boy of American soccer for Beckham? As it turned out he hadn't. Donovan had apparently given the captaincy to Beckham to encourage his integration into the side. Donovan's decision proved to be a master stroke. Beckham cajoled and urged his new team on and led by example - granted part of that example was a terribly late challenge on DC United's Jaime Moreno (Ben Olsen tagged Beckham with a hefty challenge minutes later...Beckham got up with a grin on his face).

And then the moment we had all been waiting for: a free kick outside the DC United box and Beckham stepped up. He said afterwards that he felt good as he was spotting the ball. It was the first free kick he had taken in 8 weeks and it flew past the wall and into the corner of the net. History was made and redemption, not that it was really needed, was delivered. Alexi Lalas and the LA Galaxy organization probably did a collective jig and Beckham, his team and the fans went wild. Beckham continued to urge his team forward and early in the second half set up Landon Donovan with a nice through ball. 2-0 to LA was the final score and the Beckham conquest of America was well and truly back on track.

Beckham's Call Up

In stark contrast to the negativity surrounding many English clubs, the LA Galaxy – via their President Alexi Lalas – welcomed Beckham's call up to the England team for the match with Germany.

Lalas has always seemed to intuitively understand the close and positive relationship between club and international soccer. Perhaps his own experience as an international player led to his open minded approach to Beckham flying several thousand miles for a friendly; regardless of the reason, Beckham would have been happy to hear positive comments from his boss (the fact that they are featured on Beckham's official site suggests he is!).

"We are excited that David is back on the field where he belongs. We are also excited that he has been called up by England, it is a great thing for him and he has worked so hard over the last month. It is a lot of travel, we knew that was going to happen, but if anyone can do it, he can."

Lalas seemed unconcerned that Beckham would be flying to and from England in the space of a few days and noted to the press, including Eurosport, that:

"The air travel that's involved in our league is just part of being an MLS player. Our players learn to deal with it and I'm sure David will learn to very quickly. International travel is going to be part of it."

This particular fixture, on an official FIFA international day, was scheduled in such a way that Beckham would need to fly back from England on the night of the Germany game to ensure he was available to play for the Galaxy in their cross town match against Chivas USA.

Beckham himself seemed keen to try and play both – although he noted to the press that he had not played back to back games since he was a kid. Lalas seemed to appreciate Beckham's commitment to the Galaxy cause. In his interview with *Sky Sports* he noted:

"It was never going to be ideal, but he understands that when you play these games against your city rival they are special. He was the first one to say it (flying back straight after the England game) was something he wanted to do. It was never going to be ideal, but that's the world we live in. We are never going to stand in the way of a player representing their country, but he has a domestic responsibility and he understands that."

So Beckham celebrated his first call up as a Galaxy player with a proposal that would see him play in two continents on two days while traveling thousands of miles. While it seemed that the conquest of America would exact a physical toll, Beckham clearly was reveling in being at the center of the soccer world again.

Good Deeds

Beckham the man has always had his good deeds noted but seemingly glossed over by the British press. He has always had time to turn out for charity or other "good works." He played an important role in the British Olympic bid, engaged in some important outreach work in South Africa and has been involved with global efforts to reduce the spread of malaria. As a UNICEF ambassador Beckham has worked on important causes such as malaria and HIV/AIDS for a number of years. Unfortunately those deeds have not always received the praise they deserve.

Beckham began collaborating with Malaria No More in 2006 and is featured on a terrific public service announcement that has run regularly on Fox Soccer Channel. He has been carrying the good deeds mentality to his life in the US MNM seems to be an important piece of the puzzle – it is a nonprofit organization located in New York, NY that aims to end deaths caused by malaria in Africa. It was founded in 2006 at the first ever White House Summit on Malaria by leading non-governmental organizations such as American Red Cross, UNICEF, Global Business Coalition, United Way, Millennium Promise, The Global Fund, and the United Nations Foundation. Malaria No More aims to galvanize individuals, organizations, and corporations in the private sector to provide life-saving bed nets and other critical interventions to families in need.

In addition to his work with MNM, Beckham quickly developed a good relationship with MLS WORKS and conducted important soccer outreach in the Harlem area before his first game against New York Red Bull. While these good deeds may not be central to Beckham's effort to conquer America, they do seem central to Beckham the man.

Beckham Effect Hits Giants Stadium

Over 65,000 fans crammed into Giants stadium to watch Beckham and the Galaxy square off against their home town Red Bull New York side. For any doubters, the pictures from Giants stadium should have won them over. Much like the crowd in Washington, DC the crowd had come to see David Beckham and watch their team win – they weren't disappointed.

An electric atmosphere created by the largest pro New York soccer crowd in a generation cheered their side to a stirring 5-4 win that included a hat trick from the England captain and a wonderful free kick from New York star striker Angel. The Angel goal was noteworthy because he only gave the MLS a serious look after the Beckham deal was announced at the turn of the year. The Colombian player has thrived since he joined the club and is part of the cadre of top players pulled in by the Beckham effect.

For MLS this night was the perfect storm – a terrific game from Beckham, a vocal home crowd and a wonderful game of soccer that should ensure that some of the 50,000 additional fans in Giants Stadium would be inspired to return to the stadium as soon as possible. As several commentators noted, the fans stood and screamed and cheered for their side (and Beckham) until many were hoarse. That type of energy transmitted itself onto the field and to the players. Additionally, because the game was carried live on national television, a home audience could sit back and enjoy it all. A positive cycle was created from Beckham to the fans in the stadium to the players on the pitch and the fans at home. Consequently, a lot of new fans of Red Bull and MLS were created during this game and that, surely, is what MLS wanted and had in mind when the Galaxy decided to pursue Beckham.

Ticket Controversy

Soon after David Beckham agreed to join MLS, the league authorities decided to reorient their schedule to allow fans across the country to see Beckham at least once during his shortened inaugural season. While this decision led to some grumbling among former players and a few reporters who felt it was inappropriate, most people supported the decision.

MLS clubs chose to approach their home game against Beckham in different ways with some deciding to sell the ticket for the LA Galaxy game as part of a broader package. While there were critics of this move, the clubs could rightly point out that they were ensuring that their core fans would have a better chance of seeing Beckham play (as they would be most comfortable buying such a package) and that this type of move was reasonable because the Beckham move is designed to create long lasting interest in the league. If fans ended up with tickets for non-Galaxy games they would likely attend and may end up being hooked on the core product.

Things became a bit more complicated and controversial when Beckham was injured and the clubs refused to offer refunds for tickets bought for the Galaxy game. Some fans and reporters seemed keen to push a narrative that portrayed MLS owners as short sited opportunists willing to "soak the fans" by selling tickets when the star attraction was not likely to be fit to play, or refusing to refund if he was not playing.

With all due respect, this all seems a bit silly. Does the NBA or NFL refund tickets if Shaq or Reggie Bush are unable to play due to injury? No, of course not. Fans who buy tickets take their chances in any sport and MLS should be no different. Frankly, fans in Dallas who showed up to the game between their side and the Galaxy may have missed Beckham but saw a nine goal thriller – which is certainly value for money. However, to be clear, even if the game was a 0-0 bore my opinion is the same – if you buy a ticket to see one player, any player, and he is not fit to play, you should not get a refund....go to the game and have fun....it is just sport after all.

Capello Blames Real Madrid Officials

The build up to the England v Germany game was filled with a range of interesting Beckham related pieces. Of particular note was the comment from his former coach Fabio Capello that the banishment of Beckham at Real Madrid was a board driven decision. Capello informed the Spanish paper Marca (in its print edition – with translated comments reported online by Reuters and others) that:

"The decision was taken because the club management said that he had negotiated with them having already agreed a contract with Los Angeles. They said that they couldn't count on a player that wasn't going to remain at the club."

Capello did concede that he initially backed the decision and claimed, by way of explanation, that "When I work I always wear the club shirt and defend the club in every way I can."

One interpretation of this comment from Capello is that he recognized that the continued growth of the Beckham brand made his initial decision look all the more foolish. Not only did Beckham's restoration to the Real side help their title drive, he subsequently was reinstated by England and brought his good form to the Galaxy. Did Capello feel the need to clarify why a soccer man like he would so foolishly have cast Beckham aside?

While a story such as this cannot be directly linked to Beckham's efforts in the United States, an analysis of the rationale behind Capello's comments does suggest that respected voices in the global soccer community seem ready to concede that Beckham made a good start to his LA career.

England v Germany

David Beckham has always shown a passion to play for his country and he has let the public know of his desire to reach 100 caps. Despite the tough times playing for England - most significantly his sending off against Argentina - he has always been ready to turn out for the national team.

If Beckham had to prove his desire was still strong, the effort he put into just getting to this game would be evidence enough. The former captain had to fly in from the West Coast of the United States to participate in the game.

He played well enough in the 2-1 defeat; he linked up quite effectively with young English defender Micah Richards and delivered some nice passes and through-balls. Unfortunately, the England team was lacking some confidence and in the end they were well beaten by a strong German side.

For Beckham, it was a personal triumph, back in the fold and showing commitment to the side…he played the full 90 minutes and while few took note of it, some observers could only wonder why it was necessary for the coach to keep him out there for the whole game when he had traveled so far. There was a sense that perhaps McClaren was not focused on the physical strain on Beckham the player.

Super Classico

After flying back to LA for the Super Classico, Beckham must have hoped that he could inspire his side to victory in this crunch game against their cross-town rival Chivas USA. Unfortunately things did not go to plan with the strong Chivas USA squad proving that they had more in the tank than their star studded rivals.

The game also highlighted an ongoing problem in MLS, namely the tendency of MLS referees to let some very tough tackling go without serious punishment. While the game is of course a physical one, there is a difference between tough tackling and reckless challenges that can injure players. It is vital that the MLS protect its players from the types of reckless challenges that have plagued the league.

In this game Chivas USA player Jesse Marsch was booked for taking down Beckham from behind. Beckham lost his cool because the challenge could have seriously injured him and certainly was the type of challenge that could easily have led to a red card.

So for the Galaxy overall this was a disappointing game – they lost to their closest rival 3-0, their star player was knocked around and their chances of making the play offs diminished considerably.

Hurting in the Rockies

Beckham's efforts for both club and country took their toll and he was unable to suit up for the game against the Colorado Rapids. The Galaxy, without Beckham and Donovan who had also played for club and country, could not stay in contention with the hosts and were thrashed 3-0 - hardly the best way to prepare for the game with Pachuca.

Protecting Beckham from Himself

The Super Liga final between Pachuca and the LA Galaxy was, on the one hand, a sign of good things to come for the game in North America. Unfortunately for the Galaxy they lost on penalties after a tough 120 minutes of action against a very good opponent.

The additional blow came from the fact that Beckham suffered two hard challenges and was forced to leave the field in the 33rd minute – a very worrying situation for the Galaxy.

The aftermath of Beckham's injury against Pachuta saw a considerable amount of finger pointing take place. From referees who did not give the star enough protection to the Galaxy for overplaying him (for commercial or sports reasons) to his England coach for playing him for a full 90 minutes against Germany, few escaped receiving some blame.

The one person who initially escaped blame was Beckham himself. However for anyone looking at his travel schedule and, most significantly, his playing schedule it was clear that Beckham needed to shoulder some responsibility for his injuries. He had shown an amazing passion for the game and commitment to his various teams, but the weeks leading up to the injury showed that Beckham would need to be protected from himself during the coming weeks and months.

This would not be an easy thing to achieve and a real question that came to mind was who would be able to step up and slow him down. Would it be his coach, Frank Yallop? This seemed unlikely. What about LA Galaxy President Alexi Lalas? Perhaps….but someone would need to act.

The Alter-Ego: Cuauhtémoc Blanco

When David Beckham agreed to join the LA Galaxy and MLS it quickly became apparent that his decision would have a knock on effect in the player recruitment area. By committing to the league, he immediately made it a more attractive prospect for stars from across the globe. The front office of other MLS teams immediately began reaping this specific benefit of the "Beckham Effect." Chilean legend Juan Pablo Angel's decision to join New York and Boca Juniors star Guillermo Barros Schelotto decision to swap Argentina for Columbus, Ohio, were two of the biggest names to sign on early in the season. These two, as well as the other designated players, brought something different to the game in the US and significantly contributed at the goal scoring side of the sport.

However while these stars added a great deal to the product on the field, none of them came close to matching the star power of Beckham and for some this seemed like a problem – who would join the league and become Beckham's nemesis or alter-ego? It seemed that MLS would struggle to find such a player until Cuauhtémoc Blanco agreed to join the Chicago Fire.

Suddenly in one trade MLS had a star that would help the league reach out to their already large Hispanic soccer fan base and pull them further into their orbit. While the league had certainly tried this before, this was the first time that they decided to try this using a star striker at the top of his game.

The early indications were very good with about 6000 fans coming out for Blanco's unveiling at Toyota Park. Talking to Sports Illustrated online, his new coach made clear what was expected. Juan Carlos Osorio noted:

"I hope that through my hard work and through Cuauhtémoc's talent and ability -- and that of other Hispanic players -- we can represent our community well. The most important thing is that we can contribute to the progress of the MLS. It's now a global league that is watched by many European countries, and that's something that encourages us and drives us to produce on the pitch."

Blanco did not disappoint.

He fueled his team and scored some key goals to push them into the play off picture. As Beckham sat nursing his injury in late September/early October, Blanco became a force in the league. Fans could not help wondering what would happen when he faced off with Beckham – it was certainly something to look forward to.

Tragedy and Revival

In the midst of his rehab regimen, Beckham was forced to fly home to England after his father had a heart attack. David's wife, Victoria, joined him in London. Fortunately, at the time of writing, it seems that the man who inspired David's love affair with Man United and supported his career through the years is on the way to recovery. We all wish Beckham senior a speedy and full recovery.

While Beckham eased his way back to fitness, his LA Galaxy side began to reel off a few wins in the MLS. Coach Yallop suggested that, despite the injury list, the fact that a core remained fit and able to play throughout a stretch of four games made a big difference.

Interview with Sunil Gulati

I decided to seek an interview with the President of US Soccer Sunil Gulati in order to get his impressions on the question of Beckham and more broadly on the growth of soccer in the United States – here is the full interview:

1. You were criticized in some quarters for not "delivering" a big name international coach to replace Bruce Arena. Do you feel vindicated after Bob Bradley led the national team to Gold Cup victory?

"Our goal throughout the hiring process was to find the coach best equipped to help move our national team forward, and Bob was certainly on that list from the outset. I think Bob has done a very good job of not only getting results, but laying the groundwork for the future success of this team. We all know results are important, but equally important at this stage is establishing a good foundation for the team. Already in 2007 he has used 50 different players in 14 matches, giving him a great picture of the talent available in the player pool."

2. Clearly the decision was made to prioritize the Gold Cup this summer while still trying to benefit from playing Copa America. What was the basis of the decision? Was this about ensuring the US dominates its region? Did the prize (for winning Gold Cup) of a trip to the Confederations Cup 2009 impact your thinking?

"One of our most important goals in 2007 was to win the Gold Cup and position ourselves to compete in the 2009 FIFA Confederations Cup. To play in a tournament against some of the top teams in the world, like current World Champions Italy, Brazil and others, a year before the World Cup is extremely beneficial. When you add in the fact that the tournament will serve as a dry run for South Africa 2010, the opportunity to experience the climate, stadiums, travel and other little details will be very valuable."

3. The summer after a World Cup can often be a quiet one. However, this has been a busy summer for US Soccer - a Gold Cup win, taking a young team to Copa America, David Beckham joining the LA Galaxy, the U-20 side playing well in Canada and the launch of Super Liga. Do you think that critics of the sport in the US have missed the forest for the trees?

"I'm very pleased with the how the entire year has gone. By the end of 2007, the US Men's National Team will have played 19 matches, competed in two major international tournaments, and traveled abroad five times to face a variety of quality competition. The U-20's had a very good run in Canada and showed a lot of promise. Our women's team is one of the favorites heading into the Women's World Cup in China, and the U-17 World Cup in Korea kicks off in a couple weeks. It is a very exciting time for US Soccer."

4. What are your initial impressions of David Beckham's move to MLS? What does US Soccer Federation have to do to ensure his stay has a long term positive impact on the growth of the game in the United States?

"I think Beckham brings a tremendous amount of skill and leadership on the field, and certainly a huge measure of notoriety off the field. Those things are clearly beneficial and should exist throughout David's time with the Galaxy. The goal moving forward will be to ensure that the momentum created by his coming to play in MLS endures and continues to positively impact all aspects of the sport, whether that means other good players following in his footsteps, increased media attention, improvement on the field, etc."

5. You have been clear about the fact that the US is not bidding for the 2014 World Cup but is ready to assist FIFA if a host is needed at short notice. What are the biggest challenges facing Brazil in their bid? What does the US have to do to be ready to help FIFA and host 2014 if needed?

"We have stated our intention to bid for the 2018 FIFA World Cup, and that is our focus. As we have done in the past, we are willing to assist FIFA in any way possible."

6. If Brazil does host the World Cup in 2014, the US will clearly bid for the following World Cup. What needs to happen to ensure the US is well positioned to win the bidding process?

"In 1994, the United States put on what was then the most successful World Cup in history. Since then, we have gained a tremendous amount of experience, improved our facilities, and hosted two Women's World Cups. We have a proven track record, and we are very confident that we will put forth an extremely competitive bid."

7. Adu and Altidore lit up the U-20 World Cup - what does that tell you about the future of US Soccer?

"I thought the team showed a lot of promise and played some very good soccer. Everyone was disappointed that we didn't go farther in the tournament, but the performances against Brazil and Uruguay showed a lot. Overall, I think Thomas Rongen did a good job with the group. This tournament also highlights the success that we have had with the U-17 Residency Program. Sixteen players on the roster came through Bradenton, including some of the brightest stars in the tournament, players like Freddy Adu, Josmer Altidore, Michael Bradley and Danny Szetela. These are names that could be contributing to the national team programs for many years to come, which is a hallmark of the achievements of the program. We are very proud of that, and it is why we are so excited about the establishment of the US Soccer Development Academy. The pool is only going to get bigger."

8. What are the top 3 challenges facing you and USSF over the next 12 months?

"It's not about lists and rankings. What we are doing is focusing on improving our programs across the board, increasing player development opportunities, growing our integration among all the cultures that make up the US melting pot ... and winning games. Those goals don't change."

10. What are the biggest media challenges facing the sport in the US?

"We have made solid progress in penetrating the media across all platforms, particularly in the television arena. ESPN has invested heavily in soccer, securing the rights to all of the FIFA World Cups through 2014 and paying a rights fee to both US Soccer and MLS. That demonstrates a real commitment and belief in the sport, and we are hopeful that the exposure will help continue to push soccer into the mainstream. We still face the challenge of getting consistent coverage. There remains a segment of decision makers whose generation did not grow up with the sport and will choose not to cover it over what they would call traditional sports. With the changing demographics of the country and the emergence of people in positions of authority - editors, producers, columnists - who grew up with soccer, our coverage will only continue to grow. Soccer fans are very internet savvy, and we have been well ahead of the curve in the types of coverage and access that we provide through our website. As more Americans turn to the internet to get their news and information, we should be well positioned to capitalize on it."

More Cross Over Branding: Building Brand (Reggie) Bush

Beckham has unique cross over potential in the advertising arena and is certainly able to help other big brands gain greater and more varied exposure. In the domestic sports sector New Orleans Saints running back Reggie Bush is a major brand leader. He is, however, somewhat limited on the global stage and still has room to grow in the US – enter David Beckham.

Through their joint relationship with Adidas, Beckham and Bush met for a series of one-on-one soccer and (American) football drills. This footage was featured online, in long form at various Adidas stores and in other advertisements. It was a massive success. As Darren Rovell at CNBC.COM probably recognized when he interviewed Mike Ornstein, Bush's marketing agent:

"(Rovell): It looks like the Beckham experiment for now is a bust, but what was it like for Reggie to be in that Adidas commercial with Beckham? Ornstein: The Beckham thing was very unique. About 175 million impressions was the last count I got from Adidas on worldwide exposure. We got The London Times, Bangladesh Times, there was Reggie and Beckham in places that Reggie would have never gotten to. http://www.cnbc.com/id/20622429"

Rovell was, I think, referencing Beckham's injury in the question but the real story was in the answer from Mike Ornstein when he noted that the ad had secured upwards of 175 million impressions and counting across the globe. Clearly Mike understood what Beckham had just done for Brand Bush.

From Reggie Bush to….Jon Bon Jovi

If the constructive engagement between Brand Beckham and Brand Bush is at one end of the advertising spectrum, Beckham's ability to get the critics into the news was also on display when Jon Bon Jovi lashed out at a number of pop stars (including Oasis) and Beckham in a Glamour magazine interview. The interview generated a fair bit of coverage for Jon, in part because he took a shot at Beckham, and illustrated a different way Brand Beckham can garner exposure for another brand! I'm not saying it was done with this in mind of course….but it did get picked up in the media.

Vinnie Jones Puts the Boot In

Soccer star turned actor Vinnie Jones has been living out in LA for a number of years. After reflecting on the Bon Jovi type comments, I couldn't help but notice the shots he took at the Beckham's in an interview he gave to the Daily Mail (9/15) promoting his upcoming film. Here is a piece of it:

"All the Beckham stuff… well, it's all b******s, isn't it? It really irritates me. I've seen her [Victoria] on a couple of shows already. How famous do they want to be? Just close the doors for crissakes and get on with it. I'm really pleased for David because it took some strength to get over the bad times, like when they burned effigies of him…But all this publicity is rubbish. When we played for Wimbledon , Fash [centre-forward John Fashanu] was the same, wanting to be in the papers every day. But you've got to pull back some time. I was interviewed by Victoria once for this show she was doing and she was like, "David says this" and "David says that" – trying to wind me up, I think."

Looking at this portion of the interview, it seems that Vinnie Jones falls into that ever growing category of individuals somewhat less famous than Beckham who seem to have strong opinions about him and/or his wife. Everyone is entitled to their own opinions but in this instance it is interesting to note that he did not shy away from offering an opinion when prompted.

The Backlash Against the Becklash

A number of commentators who persisted with taking shots at Beckham and the game of soccer in the US were probably surprised when a grassroots backlash against their "Becklash" started to gain momentum. For years many journalists with influence and a soap box were essentially able to treat the sport of soccer as a piniata and swing away without any criticism coming their way. I remember watching a sports awards program where the MC for the evening, a b-list actor, began with an unfunny monologue bashing the sport...I really wish he'd say that to Roy Keane's face!

Fortunately as the sport has developed in the US and with the strength of the game clearly growing, fans started to find their voice; and when Beckham was bashed by commentators and columnist's who seemingly knew little about the sport, fans reacted strongly. Perhaps the best illustration of this backlash against the "Becklash" is this letter to the editor from a soccer and Beckham fan in the Cleveland, OH area. Kevin Hignett from Bay Village chose The Plain Dealer as his venue to respond to a columnist he believed "continues to attack David Beckham, in particular, and soccer, in general, despite his glaring lack of understanding of the sport."

Mr. Hignett wrote a rather lengthy letter but the essence of his point is captured in these excerpts:

"Shaw then proceeded to...compare the effects of playing a soccer game to the effects of playing a baseball game...but how can you compare the fatigue factor of a sport where the average player runs 10K or more in 90 minutes to a sport where the average player spends about half the game sitting on his butt? Shaw also failed to point out that not only did he play three full games in six days, but that the second and third of those games were on consecutive days on two different continents!"

For too long soccer fans in the US were unwilling to do much more than stew when sports elites took jabs at their sport. The growth of soccer and the buzz created by Beckham, who gave these fans the celebrity the sport in the US needed, encouraged them to respond. The positive feelings generated around the sport were clearly spilling over from the front office of the clubs to the average fan in Middle America.

The Conquest of America Goes Online

It almost goes without saying that any sport wanting to dramatically grow its brand in the first part of the 21st Century must look to build a presence online. Most newspapers now have an online presence and soccer fans in the US and worldwide get the majority of their news from the internet. The rise of the sports blogosphere perhaps best illustrated by the growth of networks like SB Nation (full disclosure I launched SBN's first soccer blog in time for the 2006 World Cup) and the increasingly sophisticated official team sites further illustrate this growth.

Even the style of this book – a blog diary of sorts is the way I have described it – is based on this reality. I asked myself, why write a book in a style that is less comfortable to those who will want to read it. After all if we get our soccer news via blogs and short articles, surely our soccer books should try and reflect that style.

For a newer league like MLS, increasing their online presence is clearly an important piece of the puzzle from a fan base building perspective. Fortunately Beckham managed to dramatically increase the number of unique visitors to the leagues central site (www.mlsnet.com)

Several articles noted the rapid growth of traffic to the MLS hub site.

Bob Ivins, the EVP of International Markets at comScore, stated that:

"David Beckham's impact on the MLS league's official website has been enormous. The player has single handedly doubled the number of visitors to mlsnet.com versus this time last year, which let's not forget was a World Cup year."

www.MLSbet.com saw their unique visitor numbers grow from the January announcement by LA Galaxy that David Beckham had signed a five year contract. As Bizreport noted just over 800,000 people visited the soccer league website in January, 2007, 252 percent up on December 2006.

These types of numbers show that the Beckham story has the ability to reach many more people than those who will get to watch him during the MLS season. It also shows MLS that they have a real opportunity to build a relationship between their league and fans half way around the globe in places like China, Japan and Australia.

The Business of Soccer in America

In late September BusinessWeek issued its list of the 100 most powerful people in sports. Perhaps it was no huge shock that two individuals closely linked to Beckham made that group. The highest placed individual was Phil Anschutz, the Denver financier, who came in at No. 21. Among many other sports interests he does, of course, own the LA Galaxy. The survey also ranked a guy who works very closely with Phil Anschutz, Tim Leiweke, the president and CEO of Anschutz Entertainment Group. He also cracked the top half of the power list and came in at No. 42. Obviously Phil and Tim had been central to the move that saw Beckham join MLS.

Interestingly in a list that critics suggested was somewhat tilted towards the US, Beckham himself beat them both and landed at number 17 on the power list!

A key advantage of writing a blog-style book is that I can allow the thoughts of others to help fill out the mosaic. I've already shared an interview with Sunil Gulati, here is a very different interview on the Beckham effect. It is with LA Galaxy fan and blogger Mark H. Middlebrook" (http://lethalsoccer.com/)

1. What was your initial reaction when the Beckham deal was announced?

   "Beckham's arrival to the MLS was just what was needed to provide a shot in the arm to the league that was on the edge of exploding out above the ceiling placed above it in the American sports world."

2. How would you describe the atmosphere at the first game?
   Beckham's appearance at the international friendly versus Chelsea
   was full of cameras and paparazzi - a little too Hollywood in the
   beginning. However, once he was on the field and passing, his skills
   and form Proved to everyone in the Home Depot Center that he
   was worth every penny."

3. What were your thoughts when Becks smashed home his wonderful
   free kick?

   "When David bent his free kick around the defensive wall into the
   goal, it was a reminder to the fans that he is still the great player we
   anticipated and not just a new poster boy for Hollywood."

4. Looking at the season, what could the LA Galaxy management have
   done differently?

   "I think the Galaxy management allowed the hype of David's
   entrance to the MLS to cloud their better judgment that would have
   allowed him more time to heal before putting him onto the pitch.
   The greed of it all (and his desire too) to make him play before he
   was fit was a mistake."

5. Looking ahead, what should the LA Galaxy front office do better to
   increase the chances of success?

   Same response as #4

6. Are LA Galaxy fans still fully supportive of Becks?

   "Absolutely. Californian's know what Hollywood fanfare is all about
   and the rollercoaster it puts people on. I think after some of the hype
   died down and seeing how good David is in just the few minutes he's
   played, the fans just want him fit to play so we can be dazzled by his
   skills."

7. Is there another player or players LA should look to bring in to support Beckham?

   "Landon Donovan can support Beckham so long as Frank Yallop
   keeps Donovan as an attacking forward - which hasn't been the case

most of the season. Bringing someone like a Brian Ching (Houston Dynamo) or Taylor Twellman (New York Revolution) to support Beckham's service would be wonderful to see."

I also want to share the thoughts of star US soccer columnist Steve Goff of the Washington Post:

1. What was your initial reaction when you heard that the Beckham deal was completed?

   I was surprised AEG was able to actually get it done. Credit to them for pulling off the biggest deal in MLS history. Things have not turned out exactly as planned on the field, but Beckham has exposed the league to a mainstream American public that had otherwise barely heard of MLS.

2. Do you think the Galaxy has handled the media glare this season?

   They've handled it well, for the most part, from my very distant perspective. Although those in the L.A. media were probably not happy with the limited access to Beckham.

3. Do you think Beckham has managed to balance his playing and promotional commitments this season?

   Yes. The injury has obviously disrupted the overall plan.

4. Alexi Lalas suggested that the Beckham deal is on a par with the 1994 WC as a key moment for the game in the US - do you agree and do you think MLS should be looking to make another big splash next season?

   Short term, Beckham's signing had a huge impact. The 94 WC had longterm implications that we are still seeing today. So, no, I would not agree.

5. Do you think Zidane coming to the MLS/Galaxy will happen?

   No.

6. Can Beckham be an asset in the league's effort to reach the US Hispanic soccer community?

No.

7. Do you agree with the Galaxy's decision to go global by planning to go on a tour of Australia and New Zealand?

It places a lot of demands on the players, but certainly builds the Galaxy and MLS brand names. As long as the players are fairly compensated, I guess it's okay.

And here is another interesting interview with Sanjay Nayar. Sanjay is a lifelong soccer player/fan growing up in the Washington DC metro area. He has played organized soccer from the age of six and throughout High School and College. He is currently the Commissioner of the Capital Coed Soccer League (CCSL) as well as the Captain of a 2nd Division team in the League. The CCSL is a non-profit adult co-ed soccer league which has been in existence since 1994 and is one of the elite co-ed soccer leagues in the DC area with almost 1,000 players and 38 teams for the current fall season. The league is run by volunteers and is affiliated under the US Soccer Federation (USSF) and the Metropolitan D.C.-Virginia Soccer Association (MDCVA).

1. What was your initial reaction when the Beckham deal was announced?

My initial reaction was one of real excitement. I knew that such a move was in the works, but was surprised and excited to hear about the timing of the move given Beckham's involvement with the England national team and his ongoing production at the time for Real Madrid. I really could not think of an international sports figure with more mystique, appeal, and name recognition than Beckham. While there are certainly more talented international players out there, the American public would largely not have been as aware of them.

2. What do you think the Beckham deal will do for grassroots soccer?

I have seen first hand the impact that the Beckham deal has had on the MLS and more specifically the DC United crowd. There was a tangible buzz in the air around the Galaxy game which was to be one of Beckham's first showings. The great thing about the game was that even though it was only a 1-0 finish and Beckham did not do much individually, it was an incredibly exciting game with many scoring chances and my guess was that anybody who was in attendance for their first MLS game ever would leave saying, "wow that was fun – we should come back". And that is exactly the response that the league should be looking for. The game, fans, and atmosphere is as much the draw as is Beckham himself.

However, when I think of "grassroots" impact to the soccer community, I'm not sure that the deal will really have that much of an impact from the playing community. Soccer for many years has been, and will continue to be, the largest youth participation sport, and I don't see the Beckham deal will greatly influence significant change.

The one area where I think the deal will have an impact is simply for greater exposure of soccer. With MLS highlights and Beckham stories leading Sports News shows, the exposure is great for soccer for it to continue to compete with the other "Major" spectator sports and eat away at some of their market share.

3. What should MLS be doing to ensure that the Beckham deal positively impacts the grassroots?

I think the MLS has actually done a good job of this already. While many people balked at Beckham's $250M price tag, it's important to note his role not just as a player, but as a marketer and league ambassador. The league needs to be reaching out to the community not only just through Beckham but also through the other teams. Once a game with Beckham has come and gone in given cities, they need to continue the buzz through local teams or working with local soccer communities to keep the momentum going. I have witnessed this first hand with regard to our MLS/DC United's relationship with our soccer league. As one of the premier co-ed soccer leagues in the Metro Washington DC area, we have forged strong relationships with DC United who have provided discounted tickets, player meet and greets, and other promotions for us. These types of relationships do wonders for positively impacting grassroots soccer.

The league should also continue to leverage media relationships to promote soccer and the league. I have noticed an increase on ESPN with the amount of soccer highlights included in their Sportscenter. Those types of exposure are great for the league and for grassroots soccer in general. There are probably other mediums that the league could also leverage to build awareness and interest. I know many people who like to waste time going on websites such as Youtube and searching for "great soccer goals". I think that there are probably avenues like that the league could explore.

4. Looking at the season, what could the LA Galaxy management have done differently?

Won games and make the playoffs! It was an unfortunate set of circumstances with Beckham's injury/injuries and the slow start that the Galaxy had. It would have done wonders for the league had the Galaxy been more in contention. It ended up almost being a perfect scenario with their late push, but unfortunately didn't work out. One thing that the Galaxy could have done better would have been to also promote some of their other marquis players such as Landon Donovan and Cobi Jones, instead of focusing only on Beckham. In addition, his camaraderie or apparent lack there of with other players on the team also may not have sat well with fans. The US fans don't like to see prima donnas' and even if not actually the case, he may have come across as a man on an island who really hadn't integrated with his teammates.

5. Would you like to see other high profile stars join Beckham in the MLS?

Absolutely. The presence of new international players like Blanco, Angel, and Emilio has brought the league to a new level. The continued addition of international players will not only build the caliber of players in the league, but will also increase the exposure of the league to the international audience. The MLS needs to be careful, however, not to brand itself as the place that great players go to die. I think the way that the league has structured their international salary exceptions opens the door to bring in more marquis players in the primes of their careers, so it becomes a numbers game of whether the league tickets and marketing revenues can support higher salaries. I believe there will be some inertia gained with each international signing. And you can directly attribute Beckham to getting the ball rolling.

6. Has MLS made any mistakes as it tries to benefit from the Beckham effect?

I believe they rode Beckham too long. With his injury/injuries, I think it served to perpetuate soccer retractors' opinions that soccer players are "soft". Again, this was due more to unfortunate circumstances and I think they made the most of the situation by getting Beckham back on the pitch probably before he was actually ready. The buzz around his arrival was still high and I think the league would have done well to promote some of the other marquis (as noted in Q5) players along with Beckham but I didn't see much of that. They have all had major impacts to their teams and would have been marketable as well. I feel that there are 3 segments of potential MLS fans: passionate soccer fans, Sports fans who may have soccer exposure and sports fans who generally are unreachable. The Beckham deal probably has impacted the middle group the most, getting fans that wouldn't normally follow or attend an MLS game to get more interested. However, with Beckham's persona and injury, it probably started to have a negative impact to the last group who see this as case and point as the reason they don't like the sport. Aside from a US World Cup victory, I'm not sure there is much that can be done though to win over this last segment of potential fans, so I don't think the mistakes were significant.

7. What will the effect of Beckham be 5 or 10 years from now?

Beckham is coming as an ambassador to the league in the twilight of his career. I hope it will both add to the legitimacy of the league to be able to compete with other leagues around the world. We have started to see that with strong MLS showing at the Copa America and some of the friendlies with European squads. As the quality of the play increases, so does the exposure both inside and out of the US

Last year I went to a wedding in Ireland where I had a chance to speak with one of the young Irish cousins about football. A young 12 year old kid born and raised in Ireland was a rabid football (soccer) fan and out of sheer curiosity, I asked him if he was a fan or even knew of the MLS. Surprisingly he told me that he liked the Columbus Crew. I was brought back down to earth though when the reason he knew about the Crew and MLS was because of his FIFA Playstation game where in a certain career game mode, there is a point of the year where European teams are off and the MLS teams are the only ones you can play in friendlies. But hey, exposure is exposure. My hope is that with the momentum of Beckham and other international players, fans from around the world will have many more reasons to follow the MLS.

Beckham and Ricky "the Hitman" Hatton

Mid-September saw a flurry of rumors suggesting that Beckham would be asked to carry Hatton's world title belt into the ring for the fight against Floyd Mayweather.

The possibility of such a high profile guest appearance seems all the more remarkable when you consider that Beckham played for Manchester United and that Ricky "the Hitman" Hatton is a Manchester City (Citeh) supporter.

Nevertheless there is at least some discussion surrounding a possible Beckham appearance. Hatton and Mayweather's fight on December 8 at the MGM Grand in Las Vegas will determine the owner of the WBC welterweight title.

Many fans will be hoping that Hatton decides to get Beckham a key role with his entourage – can you image the Hatton fans at Las Vegas if Beckham came in with the belt and, I'm guessing, a Union Jack!

Kiwi Becks

An under reported aspect of the Galaxy's Beckham oriented marketing plan was the decision by Lalas and co. to take the team global. From Canada to Australia to the United Kingdom, teams and cities competed to attract the Galaxy to their arenas.

While there were some who questioned the decision of the Galaxy to step out of their shores, ostensibly out of concern for Beckham, others recognized what was happening. The Galaxy was projecting a confidence in their star and in their brand. They were starting to think like the super club their President stated they would be.

For those who were not convinced that David Beckham and the Galaxy would sell overseas, perhaps the best rebuttal was the prediction by Wellington City Council officials that Beckham and the Galaxy would generate six million dollars in revenue when they visited their part of New Zealand.

The deal would cost $2 million and would be contingent on a match-fit Beckham playing at least 55 minutes. The plan, as announced would see Beckham and the Galaxy remain in town for a few days staying at a central city hotel to allow fans to interact with the player's.

This type of deal seems to be the perfect model for the Galaxy and could lead to long-term growth of their brand in various parts of the globe.

My feeling is that if they continue to be strategic in their approach to touring – a game or two per trip with lots of days around to rest and recharge, the Galaxy may be able to build a decent niche for themselves in the global soccer marketplace.

FIFPro

When David Beckham was short-listed for the FIFPro's World Best XI Player Awards in late September 2007, the player and his league will have taken a moment to consider the historical significance. The global players' union had spoken when they announced their short list (55 players) and decided that a player at the height of his powers would make the list even if they played in an emerging league like the MLS. This was perhaps the perfect rebuttal to those critics who had disparaged MLS and the Galaxy by calling it the equivalent of a pub team. For Beckham, he would recognize that his objective of growing the sport in the US had taken a boost and that he and MLS could now tell players from other countries to "come to our league, you can still play at the international level and will be recognized by your peers." This short-listing was a very big piece of news.

England Dream Almost Ended Against Israel and Russia

When England prepared to play against Israel and Russia in two home quali-fiers, the fact that Beckham would be unable to contribute due to injury conjured up two different story lines. The first was the fear from an England point of view that without Beckham they would be unable to get the wins they needed to push towards qualification. The second was that Beckham's dream of reaching 100 caps for his country would also end after these games – the thinking seems to be that if England fails to qualify for Euro 2008, the team will go young looking towards South Africa 2010.

Fortunately for Beckham, his colleagues got the wins needed to keep England and his dream alive. While this was of course good news from both a national and individual standpoint, the nature of the games did raise a slightly different question.

England's coach Steve McClaren had been forced to pick some fringe players for the two key games - Gareth Barry of Aston Villa and Shaun Wright Phillips from Chelsea - and they played very well. This begged the question of whether Beckham and the injured Lampard would be able to break back into the England side for Euro 2008 if the team qualified.

Beckham watchers were probably united on this point – that for the for-mer England captain it would be a challenge he would relish.

A Conversation with Bobby Boswell

I was fortunate to be able to spend some time talking to Bobby Boswell (central defender for DC United and – I believe – future US national team starter) earlier in the week. First I should say thanks to the DC United communications department for getting me into see part of the team's training session as well as organizing the sit down chat with Bobby.

I went into the interview intending to focus on a couple of issues, the first being Bobby's impression of the Beckham effect and the second his feeling as to the potential impact of Super Liga. However, over the course of the interview I shifted gears a bit and became increasingly interested in Bobby's own future, near term, and the ramifications his philosophy would have on the way the league should plan to grow in the coming years.

First, by way of background for those of you not familiar with Bobby, he is a terrific central defender who has come a long way in a short time. From a player passed over by the league after college, Bobby entered the league as a discovery player and in 2006 became the MLS Player of the Year for his work as DC United's first choice central defender. He has also played a few games for the national team.

It's also worth pointing out that Bobby Boswell raised a few eyebrows after DC United played Beckham and the Galaxy at RFK for his impassioned critique of the way ESPN covered the game. The great Dan Steinberg covered Bobby's comments on his blog, "DC Sports bog," and the comments moved around the blogosphere pretty quickly! The money quote from Bobby's interview with Dan:

"You would think they would show the highlights of the game, but the highlights were when Beckham warmed up, when he went in, a free kick… and then they just show him kind of after the game…And my whole point is, the goal was an exciting shot, there's a red card, there's a dirty foul: that's cool.

There're a lot of chances. How do you just show him and they say, 'Oh, they lost 1-0.' What did anyone get out of that, you know what I mean?"

Early on in my interview with Bobby he made clear that the fan excitement around Beckham was good and he liked to see casual fans getting so excited by this game that he, Bobby, so clearly loves.

My impression is that Bobby is a player who thinks deeply about the game and is a guy who cares passionately both about the game in general and his role in it specifically.

He became pretty animated when we spoke about Super Liga and while he was quick to point out that it could not be compared with the Champions League due to clubs being drawn only from the US and Mexico (and in theory Canada), its potential to compound the intense international rivalry between the US and Mexican national teams is unsurpassed. He talked about how his side, DC United, just needed to keep getting themselves into positions where they could play the top sides in Mexico and that the US-Mexico club level rivalry would grow and grow in the coming years.

We spoke about his ambitions in the game and it was clear that he desperately wants to play for the US national side in the 2010 World Cup. It was also clear that he sees the best pathway to that as one that runs through European club soccer. I asked where in Europe he thinks his game would thrive and his answer, which I agree with, is that he has the ability to adapt to different leagues on the other side of the Atlantic.

For me, this aspect of the interview was particularly interesting because it suggests that, from a playing staff standpoint, MLS should not be shy about bringing in quality players like Beckham, Angel and Blanco in addition to US veterans such as Reyna and hopefully Keller and McBride while letting younger stars leave for Europe – not for the money but for the good of their education in the game.

We also chatted a bit about the way in which the US national side should play and to that Bobby described Clint Dempsey as a player who displayed the mentality and approach that best suited the US side. Bobby talked about the attitude that a player like Clint has and how that type of approach needs to be encouraged.

Finally I'd be remiss if I did not mention that Bobby had some interesting things to say about training. I had seen the second half of the training session and was really impressed by the amount of ball work, shooting work and touch play on show. I suggested that this could be because of the blend of European and Latin style play on show in MLS. Bobby corrected my assumption by observing that the session I had witnessed had far more ball work than the norm and that, in his experience, the training approach in

US soccer is far more dependant on the specific coach than any broad philosophical approach to the game.

Summing it all up I'll say that the take away from this conversation as far as Beckham and the growth of US soccer is concerned is that there are significant complexities at a player level and that they are an important dimension for the authorities to consider.

Beckham's Loyalty to the LA Galaxy

David Beckham has always displayed remarkable loyalty to the clubs he has played for despite the inevitable tensions that often swirl in and around the top clubs in the game. It is this loyalty that leads to the strong relationship both between Beckham and the fans and between Beckham and his teammates. The relationship between Beckham and the Real Madrid fans is perhaps the best illustration of the loyalty Beckham shows to his club and the way in which the public reacts to that.

With that context as a backdrop it is perhaps unsurprising that Beckham would react vocally to the bashing of his latest club by the British media.

After listening to a loud and long litany of insults directed at his new club, MLS and fans of soccer in the US, Beckham reacted strongly. In an interview with the Observer he aggressively moved to support the game in the US:

"I don't know whether it's ignorance or snobbery or whether it's that the people saying these things have never played the game or watched it being played here, but they should be sitting here now, watching us beat a team that's won the Mexican league two years running. The standard is nowhere near as low as people have been saying it is. For a start, you have to be incredibly fit and physically strong to play here: America's a country, after all, that produces some of the best athletes in the world."

Beckham also showed that he was both aware of and prepared to address the human consequences of such abuse when he noted that his coach, president and teammates were hurt when "…. people who don't know anything were turning round and calling the Galaxy a pub team and calling the MLS a Mickey Mouse league."

This type of loyalty has and always will stand Beckham in good stead. Unlike other aspects of his persona it is authentic to Beckham the man and perhaps for this reason it is something the fans that buy into Brand Beckham intuitively understand.

Bang for Your Buck with Beckham

When Alexi Lalas spoke at the annual Honda Symposium, he tackled the question of whether the Galaxy had got the most bang for their buck from David Beckham.

Interestingly Lalas felt that the club had done a pretty good job of getting the most out of Beckham off the field but were still learning how to utilize him most effectively on the field.

Lalas noted that in remarks picked up by the Associated Press and Soccernet.com: "You can plan all you want for the arrival of someone like David Beckham, but when that hurricane blows in, it is unlike anything you have ever seen. We have used it to the best of our advantage off the field. But the on-the-field aspect of it has yet to come to fruition."

Aside from the handling of the Beckham injury, it seems that this comment from Lalas is an acknowledgement of sorts that the Galaxy need to bring in better talent to support Beckham. While they do have Donovan and a few other decent players, they are perhaps lacking the one or two additional players that would allow them to get the most out of Beckham.

I will be shocked if the Galaxy does not get an enforcing midfielder to sit alongside Beckham in midfield and perhaps a rugged defender to sit behind him.

Lalas did use his speech at the event to state his belief that:

"We'll probably talk about 2007 in the way we look back at (the USA-hosted World Cup in) 1994 and say that was an important and historical moment. It's not going to be everything and we still have a long way to go, but we need to have more of these moments and more of these platforms."

While I tend to agree with this comment I feel that this season has seen some additional important platforms put in place from the recruitment of Blanco to Super Liga.

Lalas on Beckham's Possible Return for the LA Galaxy and for England?

Early October saw suggestions that Beckham would be fit for the end of season run for his club and the key Russia and Estonia games for his country. This was another issue that Alexi Lalas raised with AP and other media outlets at the annual Honda Symposium in Los Angeles. The LA Galaxy President was keen to underline that if Beckham was not fit he would not play:

"But I will tell you right now, if for one instant we feel that either physically or mentally he is not 100% ready to go, he will not play for us nor will he play for England."

The comments were sensible and frankly needed because neither Beckham nor his club and country coaches had shown, to date, that they were able to make sound judgments regarding the number of minutes the midfielder should play. Beckham, like many soccer stars wants to play all the time. Yallop and McClaren both overused him during the spell where he flew from England to LA and played 2 games in 36 hours.

It also showed an evolution in Lalas's public approach to England duty for Beckham. Whereas we had been content to speak of the Galaxy's honor when Beckham played for England, now he was quietly asserting his authority as club President with an interest in the player's health.

Nevertheless Beckham himself had clearly shown time and again his desire to play for club and country when he was less than 100% fit – would he be protected from himself?

Returning to the Fray!

As David Beckham rehabbed, the Galaxy, slowly and quietly, started to make a late run for the play offs and with two games to go and a spot in their sights, Beckham returned to action in the match against Red Bull New York. While he could not help them get the win they needed, they did get an important point in a 1-1 draw.

This set up a final game away to Blanco and the Chicago Fire. The Galaxy needed the win to advance. Unfortunately for Beckham, who came on as a sub, and the rest of the Galaxy, they could not do so and were knocked out of the play off contention when they suffered a 1-0 defeat to Chicago.

Perhaps this was for the best – Beckham and his team had worked hard but this season was not one where they looked like winning a title....but next season is a whole new ball game!

England v Croatia – Part 1

The build up to this game centered on the decisions Steve McClaren had to make from a team selection standpoint. With England only needing a draw there was a real question for the coach to grapple with. Would he put out a team designed to get that draw, a team that was built not to lose, or would he send a team out there designed to go for the win?

The formation was a key component of this decision making process. Would McClaren play with the traditional 4-4-2 system that was familiar to the majority of the England squad or would he shift to a 4-5-1 system?

A 4-4-2 system would likely see McClaren play Beckham on the right side of midfield, Gerrard and Barry in the middle of the park and Joe Cole on the left side of midfield. It would also favor a striking partnership of Peter Crouch and the diminutive striker Jermaine Defoe.

At a certain point during the course of the week, a combination of leaked reports from the camp and statements from players suggested that England would line up in a 4-5-1 formation. Peter Crouch went on the record stating that he was comfortable playing up front as the lone striker in such a system.

The other emerging feeling was that if McClaren did employ a 4-5-1 system, he would likely load the side with Chelsea players because they were more comfortable playing in that formation (largely because their former coach Jose Mourinho had employed it to good effect. Without a doubt 4-5-1 would not be in the interests of those who believed David Beckham should start.

Finally, on the eve of the match it became clear that England would in fact line up in the unusual 4-5-1 system and that the midfield 5 would include 3 players from Chelsea. Shaun Wright Phillips would replace Beckham on the right, Frank Lampard would play as part of a central 3 midfielders and Joe Cole would play on the left.

David Beckham, so often the hero for England would start on the bench (as would goalkeeper Paul Robinson – dropped for the young Scott Carson).

England v Croatia – Part 2

England started the game in disastrous fashion. Steve McClaren's decision to play the youthful Scott Carson instead of the veteran Paul Robinson backfired terribly. Portsmouth and Croatia star Nico Kranjcar fired in a speculative 30 yard shot and the Liverpool goalkeeper (on loan to Aston Villa) failed to get his body behind the ball adequately – as a consequence, when the ball bobbled slightly on the wet surface, it flew past Carson into the net. A second goal by Croatia (this one by Ivica Olic) left England with a mountain to climb and they went into the locker room 2-0 down at half-time.

Significantly, the changes in midfield had not worked either. England was missing Beckham's energy and dead ball skill in the middle of the park and they were short of firepower up front.

McClaren's hand was forced by the events of the first half and he sent on the former England captain, along with Tottenham striker Defoe to try and get back on level terms.

English fans the world over must have looked on with hope as they saw Beckham stride onto the pitch. After all he had shown a few years earlier that he could turn around critical qualifying games even when the rest of the side played poorly – who could forget his game against Greece in 2002.

In the United States, where the game was screened live on pay-per view, the legions of English fans, fans of the English game and Beckham fans alike wondered whether they would see another chapter written in Beckham's glorious career.

For a time it looked as if the ending would in fact be glorious. First Defoe won a penalty that Lampard converted for England and then Beckham sent a beautiful cross into the penalty area for Peter Crouch to smash home the tying goal. England seemed to have the draw they needed and Beckham had again provided the dramatic, fairy tale ending....or had he? In fact this time there was to be a twist in the tale and it would not be a good one for Beckham or England.

Croatian substitute Mladen Petric fired in a 25 yard shot that Scott Carson could do little about ensuring that Croatia would win 3-2 and that England would not make it to the Euro 2008 tournament.

Beckham was the last English player to leave at the end of the game – viewers wondered whether this would be the last game for his country.

England v Croatia – Part 3

The aftermath of England v Croatia was certainly filled with a fair amount of finger pointing – players past and present, senior figures in the game in England and stars from across the globe had their own theories as to why England had failed to get past Croatia and qualify for Euro 2008.

A number of theories were posited including the number of foreigners playing in the EPL and the standard of coaching utilized at the national level. A few commentators believed that the English players simply lacked the mental confidence to go out and perform to their potential. Others felt that England were technically inferior to Croatia and should not be shocked by their defeat. This last theory would be put to the test sooner rather than later as, in a surprising twist, England were promptly paired with Croatia for the qualifying stages of the 2010 World Cup (the group also included Ukraine, Belarus, Kazakhstan and Andorra).

England's former captain quickly led from the front in seeking to establish a positive mindset heading into the qualification games. Soccernet.com noted Beckham's feeling that:

"It's a group that there's still some very tough teams in and obviously Croatia's in there again and we have to try to get our own back on Croatia. But it's important that we go into the qualifiers now with a positive frame of mind…"

This type of mentality has fueled Beckham's rise to the very top of the global game and one could only help but wonder whether England would be preparing for Euro 2008 if Steve McClaren had in fact started the Galaxy midfielder.

99 Not Out

The game against Croatia had not even finished when commentators were suggesting that Beckham would end his England career on 99 caps. In the aftermath of the match a number of individuals within the game suggested that Beckham would not get the 100 caps that he has cherished for so long. Would Beckham retire? Would the Galaxy lose the cache of having an England international in their side?

Not if Beckham has anything to do with it. In the immediate aftermath of the qualification draw for World Cup 2010 Beckham made clear that he has still fully committed to the England cause. He reaffirmed his past commitment to be available for his country as long as he was playing professionally. In response to rumors of retirement or an end to his England hopes, Beckham said in Australian publication, Four Four Two, that:

"I know how things can change so quickly in the national team - eight months ago if someone would have said to me that I'd be getting another cap and playing for England I probably wouldn't have believed them. But I was brought back in and I got up to 99 caps and I want to go on from there. I believe that I can, I'm 32 years old, but I believe that I've got the experience and the passion still to play for my country. And I hope that when the next manager comes in that he gives me that chance but we'll have to wait and see."

Once again Beckham displayed the pride and commitment he has for his country, a value that resonates not just with England fans but soccer fans in the US and the world over.

A Reunion with Roy Keane?

After a story suggesting Beckham would be joining Arsenal in a loan move had been undercut by the LA Galaxy and representatives of the player himself, a new story about another loan move to the EPL kicked into high gear – this time the link was with Keane and Sunderland .

The story made little sense for a number of reasons. First, why would the LA Galaxy loan their star player out to an EPL club for a winter of soccer when Beckham is in clear need of rest before the new season? Second, after describing how happy his children are in LA, why would Beckham move either himself or the family to the North East of England for a few months during the school season and during the winter? Third, why would Beckham consider a loan move to Sunderland when he could go to virtually any team, in any league in the world?

These obvious holes in the rational did not stop a slate of Beckham links with Keane stories emerging. Fortunately both the player and his LA Galaxy coach seemed to take it in their stride. Frank Yallop wisely pointed out that this type of speculation was inevitable and that until he was told otherwise, Beckham was a Galaxy player for four more years.

Season Ends (and a new one begins) with Beckham Down Under

The LA Galaxy clearly has designs on becoming a well recognized brand both in the United States and across the globe. A key component of their global strategy is to leverage the incredible strength of the Beckham brand which is why, a few short weeks after the MLS season ended, Beckham and his Galaxy team mates found themselves playing Down Under in Australia.

The first port of call for Beckham and the Galaxy was Sydney and a friendly game against Sydney FC at the fantastic Telstra stadium. A massive crowd of 80,295 was on hand to watch a game between two teams from emerging soccer leagues, both with aspirations to join the pantheon of top European leagues.

The game certainly was one for the fans to enjoy. Sydney took an early 3-0 lead and eventually won the game 5-3. But the man they had all come to see did not disappoint his adoring public.

Beckham scored a spectacular 25 yard free kick just before half time and received a massive ovation from the crowd. He showed that he could score goals of this kind in any stadium in the world and perhaps left a few fans thinking that maybe his conquest of America would be followed up by a conquest of Australia!

While this was "merely" a promotional game, it showed how serious the Galaxy and Beckham are about developing their joint global soccer brand. Without doubt, the Beckham effect again showed how it can help build the brand identity of MLS and US soccer in general. The game – because of Beckham – was covered in the sports news from LA to the East Coast of the US and beyond. For Beckham, this was just another piece of the conquest of America.

Endnotes:

1. Lalas v the English Premier League (EPL) "Supporters" club   Donald McRae, The Guardian, • Tuesday June 19 2007 http://www.guardian.co.uk/football/2007/jun/19/newsstory.losangelesgalaxy

2. Gavin Hamilton: Dead Wrong About Beckham's Impact on Real Title Surge Gavin Hamilton, SI.Com Monday June 18 2007 http://sportsillustrated.cnn.com/2007/writers/gavin_hamilton/06/18/beckham/index.html

3. Winning over Casillas   Iam Hawkey, Sunday Times, July 17 2007 http://www.timesonline.co.uk/tol/sport/football/article1942701.ece Paul Smith, Sunday Mirror, July 17 2007 http://www.sundaymirror.co.uk/sport/football/2007/06/17/a-football-immortal---98487-19309464

4. Real Madrid and the Beckham Brand John Carlin, The Independent, February 17 2006 http://www.independent.co.uk/sport/football/news-and-comment/why-beckham-and-branding-are-key-to-reals-world-domination-466789.html

5. Beckham's Impact on Real Madrid John Carlin, The Independent, February 17 2006 http://www.independent.co.uk/sport/football/news-and-comment/why-beckham-and-branding-are-key-to-reals-world-domination-466789.html

6. The Real deal: Beckham's effect John Carlin, The Times, September 19 2004 http://www.timesonline.co.uk/tol/sport/football/arti-

cle484417.ece and a block quote here: Iam Hawkey, Sunday Times, July 17 2007 http://www.timesonline.co.uk/tol/sport/football/european_football/article1948101.ece

7. Deloitte February 16 2006 http://www.deloitte.com/dtt/press_release/0,1014,sid%253D2834%2526cid%253D109830,00.html

8. Galaxy v Chivas of Guadalajara AP July 30 2007 http://msn.foxsports.com/soccer/story/7071004?CMP=OTC-K9B1408813162&ATT=176 John Nisbet, The Independent, July 30 2007

9. Pele DEAN McNULTY -- **Sun Media August 1 2007** http://slam.canoe.ca/Slam/Soccer/TorontoFC/2007/08/01/4385184-sun.html (via interview with Frankfurter Allgemeine Sonntagszeitung)

10. Dale Earnhardt Jr. and Tiger Respect Beckham AP, July 11 2007 http://nbcsports.msnbc.com/id/19709738/ The Times, August 8 2007 and Tom Watt Observer Monthly September 2 2007

11. DC United v LA Galaxy (August 9 2007) Michael Wilbon, Washington Post, August 10 2007 http://www.washingtonpost.com/wp-dyn/content/article/2007/08/09/AR2007080902422.html and Australian Four Four Two August 10 2007 http://au.fourfourtwo.com/news/58654,beckham-pleased-to-end-frustrating-wait.aspx and http://davidbeckham.fans-online.com/2007_08_01_archive.html (Ben Olsen quote)

12. New England and the Critics AP story carried at http://wbztv.com/topstories/David.Beckham.New.2.589157.html

13. Beckham Backlash Phil Gordos August 16 2007 BBC online http://news.bbc.co.uk/sport2/hi/football/6947328.stm

14. **"Meanwhile: Beckham hype won't play in the US" Alex Beam Boston Globe August 16 2007** http://www.iht.com/articles/2007/08/16/opinion/edbeam.php

15 Lalas on Beckham Schedule Euro Sport Aug 17 2007 and also references Sky Sports http://uk.eurosport.yahoo.com/17082007/4/lalas-reveals-beckham-schedule.html

16. Capello Blames Real Madrid Officials Marca (print) Wednesday 22 August 2007 via http://allinwhite.blogspot.com/2007/08/capello-lashes-out.html#links

17. The Alter-Ego: Cuauhtémoc Blanco Grant Wahl Sports Illustrated online August 27 2007 http://sportsillustrated.cnn.com/2007/writers/grant_wahl/08/27/blanco/1.html

18. More Cross Over Branding: Building Brand (Reggie) Bush Darren Rovell Sports Biz Thursday, 6 Sep 2007 http://www.cnbc.com/id/20622429

19. Vinnie Jones Puts the Boot In Lina Das September 15 2007 Daily Mail http://www.dailymail.co.uk/moslive/article-480523/The-riddle-Vinnie-Jones.html

20. The Backlash Against the Becklash Cleveland Plain Dealer Letters Page http://www.cleveland.com/plaindealer/lettertoeditor.ssf

21. The Conquest of America Goes Online Com Score August 30 2007 http://www.comscore.com/press/release.asp?press=1598

22. The Business of Soccer in America Business Week Lowry and Keating September 25, 2007 http://www.businessweek.com/bwdaily/dnflash/content/sep2007/db20070925_346159.htm?chan=top+news_special+report+--+the+power+100_special+report+

23. Observer Sports Monthly, 31 August http://observer.guardian.co.uk/osm/story/0,,2159911,00.html AFP Sept 2 2007 carrying Observer story http://afp.google.com/article/ALeqM5jcH3Gqs6MH0uwfJF-a_-ZFojrtfw

24. Bang for Your Buck with Beckham Oct 5 2007 http://soccernet.espn.go.com/news/story?id=469785&

25. England v Croatia – Part 3 **4thegame.com** http://www.4thegame.com/features/feature/211015/beckhamwatch_becks_bends_it_down_under.html

26. 99 Not Out **4thegame.com** http://www.4thegame.com/features/feature/211015/beckhamwatch_becks_bends_it_down_under.html